Just For You

A Daily Self-Care
JOURNAL

Happy
Healthy
Caregiver

Elizabeth B. Miller

*"These empty pages
are your future,
soon to become your past.
It will read
the most personal tale
you shall ever find
in a book."*

—Anonymous

this Journal belongs to:

_____

ABOUT THIS JOURNAL

Congratulations for taking a valuable step in your personal self-care journey. My intent for creating this journal was to give people a tool that would help them prioritize their daily self-care. I personally love journals and have found writing to be so cathartic. I like to say that when I am more transparent with my thoughts and feelings, I see myself more clearly.

I've seen first-hand the impact that neglecting self-care has had on several people I love. I've been a family caregiver for over 10 years to my parents. I've seen how the choices they made to care for everyone else and put themselves last not only impacted their own health and happiness but truly affected everyone around them.

When my dad passed in 2014 at the age of 76 and I became the primary caregiver for my mom, I knew I must choose a different path for me and my immediate family. I had to make some changes in my life to break the cycle. Putting focus on my personal health and happiness was easier said than done as I had a full-time career, a partner who was also a primary caregiver for his mom, two active teenagers, and brand new caregiving responsibilities.

The first thing I did to help me adopt this new self-care mindset was commit to posting something on Instagram daily (#100DaysofHealthy). Process improvement is an important skill I use in my career. I began doing some process improvement in my own life looking for small ways to integrate self-care into my days. The crazy thing was that I wasn't only feeling better but I experienced more energy to be able to give to others.

In February 2015, I started my online business to support family caregivers. I couldn't keep this message all to myself and at the time I wasn't finding the support I needed online. I saw a need to publically disrupt the 'norm' (i.e. taking care of everyone else and worrying about your own needs last). However, I not only wanted to flip this basic behavior upside down but I needed to share my journey along the way to give others an example of what a caregiving life with integrated self-care could look like. The resources and messages I share on my website and in the Happy Healthy Caregiver podcast are pragmatic. I want to share not only how I'm finding small ways to integrate self-care but shine a spotlight on others who are working on their health and happiness, as well.

I'm so excited for the journey the pages in this journal will be taking you on. I can't wait to hear how being intentional about your daily self-care is having a positive ripple effect on your life and those around you.

Happy journaling!

Elizabeth

elizabeth@happyhealthycaregiver.com

JANUARY 1

What's one of your goals for yourself this year?

_____

_____

_____

_____

_____

_____

_____

_____

_____

_____

_____

_____

_____

_____

_____

_____

_____

_____

JANUARY 2

How do you recover from a tough day?

JANUARY 3

What was your favorite activity to do
as a child?

JANUARY 4

What is the last thing you did that made you happy?

_____

_____

_____

_____

_____

_____

_____

_____

_____

_____

_____

_____

_____

_____

_____

_____

_____

_____

_____

_____

JANUARY 5

When do you feel your healthiest?

_____
_____
_____
_____
_____
_____
_____
_____
_____
_____
_____
_____
_____
_____
_____
_____
_____
_____
_____

_____

_____

_____

_____

_____

_____

_____

_____

_____

_____

_____

_____

_____

_____

_____

_____

_____

_____

JANUARY 6

Your life
could feel
less rushed if...

_____

_____

_____

_____

_____

_____

_____

_____

_____

_____

_____

_____

_____

_____

_____

_____

_____

JANUARY 7

What are you
most grateful for right now?

JANUARY 8

What's your favorite thing about winter?

_____
_____
_____
_____
_____
_____
_____
_____
_____
_____
_____
_____
_____
_____
_____
_____

JANUARY 9

What's the most exciting thing
happening in your life right now?

_____

_____

_____

_____

_____

_____

_____

_____

_____

_____

_____

_____

_____

_____

_____

_____

_____

_____

_____

_____

_____

_____

_____

_____

_____

_____

_____

_____

_____

_____

_____

_____

_____

_____

_____

_____

_____

_____

_____

JANUARY 10

What do you value most in a
friendship?

JANUARY 11

Share five to ten items
on your bucket list.

JANUARY 12

List the products you would include
in a self-care tote bag.

_____

_____

_____

_____

_____

_____

_____

_____

_____

_____

_____

_____

_____

_____

_____

_____

_____

_____

_____

JANUARY 13

If you could have
only one self-care product
on a desert island,
it would be . . .

_____

_____

_____

_____

_____

_____

_____

_____

_____

_____

_____

_____

_____

_____

_____

_____

_____

_____

_____

JANUARY 14

If you had an hour to do
whatever you want
what would you do?

ZZZ

JANUARY 15

At this moment, what words would you most like to hear from other people?

JANUARY 16

How do you calm yourself when you
feel anxious?

_____

_____

_____

_____

_____

_____

_____

_____

_____

_____

_____

_____

_____

_____

_____

_____

_____

_____

_____

JANUARY 17

What's your favorite exercise to do to break a sweat?

_____

_____

_____

_____

_____

_____

_____

_____

_____

_____

_____

_____

_____

_____

_____

_____

_____

_____

_____

_____

_____

JANUARY 18

What might it feel like
for you to be the person
receiving help
versus giving it?

_____

_____

_____

_____

_____

_____

_____

_____

_____

_____

_____

_____

_____

_____

_____

_____

_____

JANUARY 19

What would your
perfect day look like?

JANUARY 20

If you could take a year off and go anywhere in the world, where would you go?

_____

_____

_____

_____

_____

_____

_____

_____

_____

_____

_____

_____

_____

_____

_____

_____

_____

JANUARY 21

Describe a quality you most admire in other people.

_____

_____

_____

_____

_____

_____

_____

_____

_____

_____

_____

_____

_____

_____

_____

_____

_____

_____

JANUARY 22

How do you want
to be remembered
by your family?

_____

_____

_____

_____

_____

_____

_____

_____

_____

_____

_____

_____

_____

_____

_____

_____

_____

JANUARY 23

What are your signs
that you may be
lacking in self-care?

JANUARY 24

Something that you could buy
that would get you excited
about your health is . . .

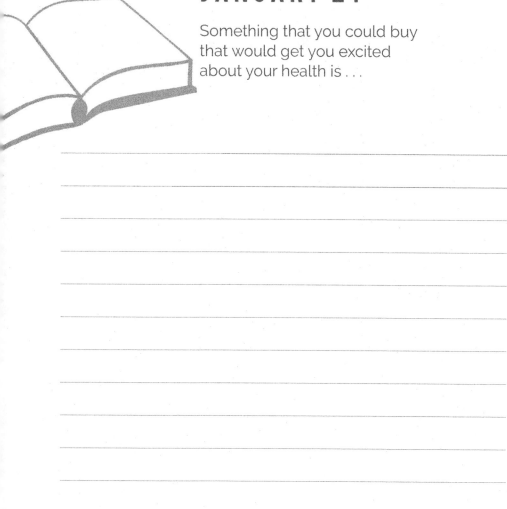

JANUARY 25

Who would you call to have a lunch date with this week?

hello

_____

_____

_____

_____

_____

_____

_____

_____

_____

_____

_____

_____

_____

_____

_____

_____

_____

_____

JANUARY 26

You have one hour
to catch up with a
friend or family member,
who would you call?

JANUARY 27

It's your last night on Earth
... what would your
last supper look like?

JANUARY 28

What are you reading right now?

_____

_____

_____

_____

_____

_____

_____

_____

_____

_____

_____

_____

_____

_____

_____

_____

_____

_____

_____

JANUARY 29

What's your favorite guilty pleasure?

_____

_____

_____

_____

_____

_____

_____

_____

_____

_____

_____

_____

_____

_____

_____

_____

_____

_____

_____

JANUARY 30

What's one unhealthy habit
you have successfully kicked?

_____

_____

_____

_____

_____

_____

_____

_____

_____

_____

_____

_____

_____

_____

_____

_____

_____

JANUARY 31

What's your
favorite feature
about your body?

FEBRUARY 1

What makes you feel cozy?

_____

_____

_____

_____

_____

_____

_____

_____

_____

_____

_____

_____

_____

_____

_____

_____

_____

_____

_____

_____

FEBRUARY 2

What's an exercise
or sport that you
would like to try?

FEBRUARY 3

What's a song you play
to get yourself
in a good mood?

FEBRUARY 4

If you could meet
any fictional character
it would be . . .

_____

_____

_____

_____

_____

_____

_____

_____

_____

_____

_____

_____

_____

_____

_____

_____

_____

_____

_____

_____

FEBRUARY 5

What celebrity would you choose to spend the day with and why?

FEBRUARY 6

What's one thing
about life you wish
someone had told you?

_____
_____
_____
_____
_____
_____
_____
_____
_____
_____
_____
_____
_____
_____
_____
_____

FEBRUARY 7

Among your friends,
who reenergizes you the most?

FEBRUARY 8

What's a new restaurant
you've been wanting to try?

FEBRUARY 9

What's one of your favorite
smartphone apps?

FEBRUARY 10

Which celebrity
would you want
to play the role
of you in your life?

_____

_____

_____

_____

_____

_____

_____

_____

_____

_____

_____

_____

_____

_____

_____

_____

_____

_____

FEBRUARY 11

What's one activity that drains you
that you could delegate to another
person?

FEBRUARY 12

What's one thing you are saving for a
rainy day?

FEBRUARY 13

If you could wave a magic wand and change one thing about your life, what would it be?

_____

_____

_____

_____

_____

_____

_____

_____

_____

_____

_____

_____

_____

_____

_____

_____

_____

_____

_____

_____

_____

_____

_____

_____

_____

_____

_____

_____

_____

_____

_____

_____

_____

_____

_____

_____

_____

_____

_____

FEBRUARY 14

What do you love
most about your life
right now?

FEBRUARY 15

What is one of your
favorite quotes?

FEBRUARY 16

Who can you count on
to make you laugh?

FEBRUARY 17

What's the healthiest item in your fridge right now?

FEBRUARY 18

When you're in pain,
the kindest thing
you could do for yourself
would be . . .

FEBRUARY 19

What was the last thing
that happened
that made you
laugh out loud?

FEBRUARY 20

When is the last time you asked
someone for help?

FEBRUARY 21

If you started a business of your own,
what would it be?

_____

_____

_____

_____

_____

_____

_____

_____

_____

_____

_____

_____

_____

_____

_____

_____

_____

FEBRUARY 22

What are
three positive adjectives
you would use
to describe yourself?

FEBRUARY 23

What's your
current go-to healthy lunch?

FEBRUARY 24

Who is a person that inspires you to want to be the best version of yourself?

_____

_____

_____

_____

_____

_____

_____

_____

_____

_____

_____

_____

_____

_____

_____

_____

_____

_____

_____

FEBRUARY 25

The best time in your day
to practice self-care is . . .

_____
_____
_____
_____
_____
_____
_____
_____
_____
_____
_____
_____
_____
_____
_____
_____
_____
_____
_____

FEBRUARY 26

If money were no object,
what would you
buy for yourself?

_____

_____

_____

_____

_____

_____

_____

_____

_____

_____

_____

_____

_____

_____

FEBRUARY 27

What is something
you are currently
doing right?

FEBRUARY 28

If you could save one photo from your
childhood which one would it be?

FEBRUARY 29

Describe a moment in time where you took a leap of faith?

How did it turn out for you?

Self-Care
BINGO

B	I	N	G	O
15 minute walk	Cut up fruits or veggies for the week	Download meditation app & try a guided meditation	Call a friend just to chat (make it a 'twofer' if you can walk & talk)	Write a paragraph about your day
Meet a friend for lunch or dinner	Get 7 hours of sleep or take a nap	Complete an online yoga session	Listen to uplifting music while running errands & completing tasks	Unfollow accounts on social media that don't make you feel good
Clean out a drawer or closet or email inbox	Listen to an episode of an uplifting podcast	★ FREE	Try a new healthy recipe	Enjoy an afternoon cup of tea or coffee
Watch a funny online video	Read a chapter of a book	Relax for 15 minutes in the sunshine	Make arrangements for a few hours of fun	Tuck a few healthy snacks in your car or purse
Drink 64oz of water today	Spend a day unplugged from social media	Create a list of 5 or more things you are grateful for	Complete an online workout	Read the nutrition labels on everything you can today

MARCH 1

What movie or TV show could you turn to for a guaranteed laugh?

_____

_____

_____

_____

_____

_____

_____

_____

_____

_____

_____

_____

_____

_____

_____

_____

_____

_____

_____
_____
_____
_____
_____
_____
_____
_____
_____
_____
_____
_____
_____
_____
_____
_____
_____
_____

MARCH 2

What's your favorite
self-care activity
that doesn't cost a penny?

_____

_____

_____

_____

_____

_____

_____

_____

_____

_____

_____

_____

_____

_____

_____

_____

MARCH 3

What's one item in your home that
makes you happy?

MARCH 4

What's your current go-to healthy breakfast?

_____

_____

_____

_____

_____

_____

_____

_____

_____

_____

_____

_____

_____

_____

_____

_____

_____

_____

_____

_____

MARCH 5

What's your favorite thing about spring?

_____
_____
_____
_____
_____
_____
_____
_____
_____
_____
_____
_____
_____
_____
_____
_____
_____
_____
_____
_____
_____
_____

MARCH 6

What story from your past is your
favorite story to tell?

_____

_____

_____

_____

_____

_____

_____

_____

_____

_____

_____

_____

_____

_____

_____

_____

_____

_____

_____

_____

_____

_____

MARCH 7

What is your favorite prayer or phrase
that makes you feel calm?

MARCH 8

If you were an animal, you'd choose to be a . . . because . . .

MARCH 9

What's the bravest thing you have ever done by yourself?

_____

_____

_____

_____

_____

_____

_____

_____

_____

_____

_____

_____

_____

_____

_____

_____

_____

_____

MARCH 10

How do you manage stress?

_____
_____
_____
_____
_____
_____
_____
_____
_____
_____
_____
_____
_____
_____
_____
_____

MARCH 11

What's standing
in the way of
putting your health first?

MARCH 12

How many hours of sleep are you averaging lately?

What's preventing you from getting the sleep you need?

_____

_____

_____

_____

_____

_____

_____

_____

_____

_____

_____

_____

_____

_____

_____

_____

_____

MARCH 13

What is your most favorite healthy homemade dish that brings you comfort?

_____

MARCH 14

What would you do
if the internet was
broken for 3 days?

MARCH 15

What's one local attraction
you have been
meaning to visit
but haven't yet?

MARCH 16

How do you keep the romance alive in your relationship?

_____
_____
_____
_____
_____
_____
_____
_____
_____
_____
_____
_____
_____
_____
_____
_____
_____
_____
_____
_____
_____

MARCH 17

How have you been lucky in life?

_____

_____

_____

_____

_____

_____

_____

_____

_____

_____

_____

_____

_____

_____

_____

_____

_____

_____

_____

_____

_____

_____

MARCH 18

What would
you choose
for your karaoke song?

_____

_____

_____

_____

_____

_____

_____

_____

_____

_____

_____

_____

_____

_____

_____

_____

_____

_____

_____

MARCH 19

What's your
favorite physical attribute?

MARCH 20

When was the last time you were in 'awe' of something?

_____

_____

_____

_____

_____

_____

_____

_____

_____

_____

_____

_____

_____

_____

_____

_____

_____

_____

_____

MARCH 21

What's on your to-do list right now
that is important but not urgent?

_____

_____

_____

_____

_____

_____

_____

_____

_____

_____

_____

_____

_____

_____

_____

_____

_____

_____

_____

MARCH 22

Even when you're overwhelmed,
stressed or upset,
you can't help but smile or laugh
when you see . . .

_____

_____

_____

_____

_____

_____

_____

_____

_____

_____

_____

_____

_____

_____

_____

MARCH 23

What object
in your home
brings you comfort?

MARCH 24

What's the last charity you donated
time or money to?

_____

_____

_____

_____

_____

_____

_____

_____

_____

_____

_____

_____

_____

_____

_____

_____

_____

_____

MARCH 25

What is one of your favorite scents?

MARCH 26

What project
are you looking forward
to starting?

MARCH 27

What project
are you looking
forward to completing?

MARCH 28

Even though you may not be able to change your situation, one thing you could do to take a step in the right direction would be to . . .

_____

_____

_____

_____

_____

_____

_____

_____

_____

_____

_____

_____

_____

_____

_____

_____

_____

MARCH 29

What activity are you currently doing
that drains your energy?

_____
_____
_____
_____
_____
_____
_____
_____
_____
_____
_____
_____
_____
_____
_____
_____
_____
_____
_____

_____

_____

_____

_____

_____

_____

_____

_____

_____

_____

_____

_____

_____

_____

_____

_____

_____

_____

_____

_____

MARCH 30

What is most meaningful
to you right now?

_____

_____

_____

_____

_____

_____

_____

_____

_____

_____

_____

_____

_____

_____

_____

_____

_____

_____

MARCH 31

What is your
favorite time of day
and why?

songs that
make my heart
SING

APRIL 1

What system could you put in place to schedule your self-care activities?

_____

_____

_____

_____

_____

_____

_____

_____

_____

_____

_____

_____

_____

_____

_____

_____

_____

_____

_____

_____

_____

_____

_____

_____

_____

_____

_____

_____

_____

_____

_____

_____

_____

_____

_____

_____

_____

_____

_____

APRIL 2

How do you stay
in the present moment?

_____

_____

_____

_____

_____

_____

_____

_____

_____

_____

_____

_____

_____

_____

_____

_____

_____

_____

APRIL 3

If you were a Disney character, who
would you be?

APRIL 4

If you could change one thing about
your present life it would be . . .

APRIL 5

What's one change you'd like to make
to your diet or exercise regime?

APRIL 6

What's the last
good movie you saw?

_____

_____

_____

_____

_____

_____

_____

_____

_____

_____

_____

_____

_____

_____

_____

_____

APRIL 7

What is something
you are trying to let go of?

APRIL 8

What's a day trip adventure you've been wanting to take?

APRIL 9

How do you unwind before bedtime?

_____

_____

_____

_____

_____

_____

_____

_____

_____

_____

_____

_____

_____

_____

_____

_____

_____

_____

_____

_____

APRIL 10

Where would you go
if you won
a dream vacation?

_____
_____
_____
_____
_____
_____
_____
_____
_____
_____
_____
_____
_____
_____
_____

APRIL 11

What's one thing you could do in your
home or work environment that would
help reduce stress or anxiety?

APRIL 12

What hobby do you most enjoy doing?

APRIL 13

What relaxation strategy
helps you the most?

APRIL 14

What have you
done lately
that makes
you proud of yourself?

ZZZ

_____

_____

_____

_____

_____

_____

_____

_____

_____

_____

_____

_____

_____

_____

APRIL 15

What was the
last thing you said no to?

APRIL 16

What's one nice thing that happened today?

APRIL 17

The words you need to hear right now are . . .

hello

_____

_____

_____

_____

_____

_____

_____

_____

_____

_____

_____

_____

_____

_____

_____

_____

_____

_____

_____

APRIL 18

How do you
unplug from
technology?

_____

_____

_____

_____

_____

_____

_____

_____

_____

_____

_____

_____

_____

_____

_____

_____

_____

_____

APRIL 19

What was
one of your
big wins this week?

APRIL 20

If you wrote a book (or another book!) what would it be about?

APRIL 21

What's the source of your current stress?

_____

_____

_____

_____

_____

_____

_____

_____

_____

_____

_____

_____

_____

_____

_____

_____

_____

APRIL 22

What would the
movie title
for your life be right now?

_____

_____

_____

_____

_____

_____

_____

_____

_____

_____

_____

_____

_____

_____

_____

APRIL 23

What's the most
amazing tech gadget
you've discovered
to help you?

APRIL 24

What are you planning to do for fun
next weekend?

_____

_____

_____

_____

_____

_____

_____

_____

_____

_____

_____

_____

_____

_____

_____

_____

_____

APRIL 25

What is something you wish you knew more about?

_____

_____

_____

_____

_____

_____

_____

_____

_____

_____

_____

_____

_____

_____

_____

_____

_____

_____

_____

_____

APRIL 26

What's one happy memory
related to childhood you have?

Why do you think
this memory stands out?

APRIL 27

What's your
favorite character trait?

APRIL 28

What is your secret truth about happiness?

APRIL 29

You practice self-care
because you want to feel . . .

_____

_____

_____

_____

_____

_____

_____

_____

_____

_____

_____

_____

_____

_____

_____

_____

_____

APRIL 30

What is your
top tip to bust stress?

MAY 1

How are you feeling today?

MAY 2

If you could take a whole day off, how would you spend it?

_____

_____

_____

_____

_____

_____

_____

_____

_____

_____

_____

_____

_____

_____

_____

_____

_____

_____

_____

MAY 3

When you envision your future . . .
what do you see?

MAY 4

What helps you deal with the difficult challenges life brings your way?

MAY 5

Describe an embarrassing moment in your life.

_____

_____

_____

_____

_____

_____

_____

_____

_____

_____

_____

_____

_____

_____

_____

_____

_____

_____

_____

_____

_____

_____

_____

_____

_____

_____

_____

_____

_____

_____

_____

_____

_____

_____

_____

_____

_____

_____

_____

_____

_____

MAY 6

What unexpected blessing
have you recently received?

_____

_____

_____

_____

_____

_____

_____

_____

_____

_____

_____

_____

_____

_____

_____

_____

_____

_____

_____

MAY 7

What's one thing you admire about
your family?

MAY 8

What is your mantra that is currently
keeping you motivated?

MAY 9

When you are older
and need care,
what do you hope
someone does for you?

_____

_____

_____

_____

_____

_____

_____

_____

_____

_____

_____

_____

_____

_____

_____

_____

_____

_____

_____

_____

_____

_____

_____

_____

_____

_____

_____

_____

_____

_____

_____

_____

_____

_____

_____

_____

_____

_____

MAY 10

What's your
current favorite outfit
to wear?

_____

_____

_____

_____

_____

_____

_____

_____

_____

_____

_____

_____

_____

_____

_____

_____

_____

MAY 11

What is a lesson you have learned
from a family member or friend?

MAY 12

What is your favorite holiday and why?

MAY 13

What is the main thing weighing on your mind today?

MAY 14

What's one
unhealthy food
you could substitute
with a healthy food
replacement?

_____

_____

_____

_____

_____

_____

_____

_____

_____

_____

_____

_____

_____

_____

_____

_____

_____

MAY 15

What energizes you right now?

MAY 16

What are you doing to share the
family responsibilities?

_____

_____

_____

_____

_____

_____

_____

_____

_____

_____

_____

_____

_____

_____

_____

_____

_____

_____

MAY 17

Do you currently feel isolated? What's one thing you could do to remedy this feeling?

_____

_____

_____

_____

_____

_____

_____

_____

_____

_____

_____

_____

_____

_____

_____

_____

_____

_____

_____

_____

_____

_____

_____
_____
_____
_____
_____
_____
_____
_____
_____
_____
_____
_____
_____
_____
_____
_____
_____

MAY 18

What's a small random
act of kindness
you could do this week
for a complete stranger?

_____

_____

_____

_____

_____

_____

_____

_____

_____

_____

_____

_____

_____

_____

_____

_____

_____

_____

_____

_____

_____

MAY 19

Who do you envy
& what could you incorporate
into your life that they have?

MAY 20

If you could go anywhere in the world, where would you go?

_____

_____

_____

_____

_____

_____

_____

_____

_____

_____

_____

_____

_____

_____

_____

_____

_____

_____

MAY 21

What local attraction have you never visited but want to?

_____
_____
_____
_____
_____
_____
_____
_____
_____
_____
_____
_____
_____
_____
_____
_____
_____
_____
_____
_____
_____
_____

MAY 22

What's a topic
that interests you
that you would like to
learn more about?

_____

_____

_____

_____

_____

_____

_____

_____

_____

_____

_____

_____

_____

_____

_____

MAY 23

What's the best
non-fiction book
you've ever read?

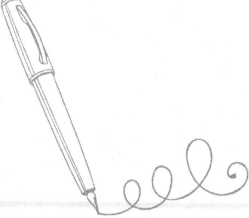

MAY 24

What's the best fiction book you've ever read?

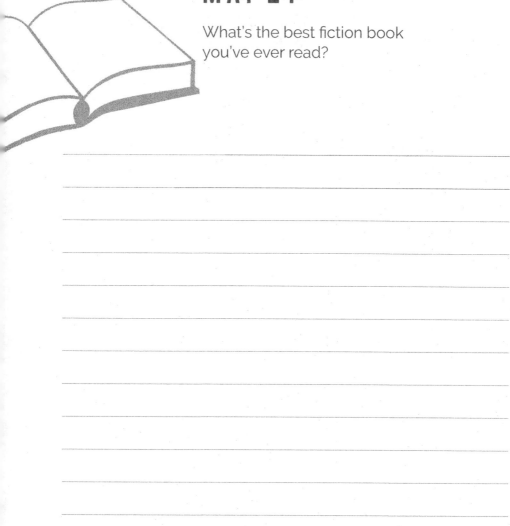

MAY 25

What activity did you do as a child that brought you great joy?

_____

_____

_____

_____

_____

_____

_____

_____

_____

_____

_____

_____

_____

_____

_____

_____

_____

_____

_____

_____

_____

_____

_____

_____

_____

_____

_____

_____

_____

_____

_____

_____

_____

_____

_____

_____

_____

_____

MAY 26

What's something good
that happened this week
that was unexpected?

_____

_____

_____

_____

_____

_____

_____

_____

_____

_____

_____

_____

_____

_____

MAY 27

What are you doing
to prevent 'losing yourself'
while caring for others?

MAY 28

What small area of your house
has the potential to bring you joy?

_____

_____

_____

_____

_____

_____

_____

_____

_____

_____

_____

_____

_____

_____

_____

_____

_____

_____

MAY 29

What is one past experience that you
know you need to let go of?

_____

_____

_____

_____

_____

_____

_____

_____

_____

_____

_____

_____

_____

_____

_____

_____

_____

_____

_____

MAY 30

Who do you lean on
for support?

_____

_____

_____

_____

_____

_____

_____

_____

_____

_____

_____

_____

_____

_____

_____

_____

_____

_____

MAY 31

How do you celebrate
your personal successes?

Self-Care
WORD SEARCH

```
G Q I L Y C C I F R J O C U P N X G H D S I W U Y
Z M U S I C D N C L J U M R Z L B N J O Z R V G Q
S O Z F S L C Y N B V W M I N D F U L N E S S R Z
H E A L T H Y Z R S W E E I D N I L B Y U J Z S A
O G Q Q T G O P K G V U L P R L N U T R I T I O N
N S V L G A D F C G W Y Z R T O I N Q V U J T B O
N E E X Z Y V F C E K V H S H I O V D T J H H V E
X L B P G I Q I C P C O M P A S S I O N W Z Z Q Y
Q F S L Z R G U G H V F P D O Z L Q U V S B G D V
N C H H G Y A I Y U O T R L A U G H T E R M A R Y
T A O Q X W F T N K I B S I S L D N M K G L S E N
P R U Y M P X Z I T C E B Q E Y D Z X O X L K A A
U E K Y O F H U Z T E P F I R N T C G T U B F M K
O K T D V J T S B L U N Q I E P D O N J G O O S P
B P P F E F D S C H Y D T R B S O S K N Y D R O S
V Z P T M O I K S U A X E I I H T F E C P Y H R K
E M T U E K C Q L W M P V Y O S W N N W N I E S J
Y S X U N T A S E T V I P B X N Y I A H I M L A K
U U V R T J L G E M A B C I W J A M B A M A P S Q
A P J R D I M G P O O S B Y N O B L O A U G B B V
Y P H I B U A C O Y U J R S A E B O V L Z E E Z I
M O O C S B S D S M Z T Q K K Z S D D V Z L Q O H
G R W B M R Q E D P R S D N D N R S M J R U U G M
W T M J O I Q P K O B W Y X U C Q X P L A M Y E P
R A M J I L C F Q H M D X D K E R U N P L U G Z R
```

intentional   mindfulness   ask for help   compassion
body-image   nutrition   gratitude   happiness
self-care   movement   hobbies   laughter
healthy   friends   support   unplug
sleep   music   dreams   calm

JUNE 1

What activity could you do that combines physical movement with spending time with someone (a 'twofer'!)?

_____

_____

_____

_____

_____

_____

_____

_____

_____

_____

_____

_____

_____

_____

_____

_____

_____

_____

_____

_____

_____

_____

_____

_____

_____

_____

_____

_____

_____

_____

_____

_____

_____

_____

_____

JUNE 2

If you were to lose all your possessions
what item would you miss the most?

_____

_____

_____

_____

_____

_____

_____

_____

_____

_____

_____

_____

_____

_____

_____

JUNE 3

What's a fruit or vegetable that you
have never tried before?

JUNE 4

What's one thing you accomplished this week that wasn't listed on your to-do list?

JUNE 5

The funniest movie
you have ever seen was . . .

_____

_____

_____

_____

_____

_____

_____

_____

_____

_____

_____

_____

_____

_____

_____

_____

_____

_____

_____
_____
_____
_____
_____
_____
_____
_____
_____
_____
_____
_____
_____
_____
_____
_____
_____
_____
_____

JUNE 6

What five adjectives
do you think
others would give
to describe you?

JUNE 7

What life accomplishment
makes you proud?

JUNE 8

What's your favorite vacation spot?

_____

_____

_____

_____

_____

_____

_____

_____

_____

_____

_____

_____

_____

_____

_____

_____

_____

_____

_____

JUNE 9

What's the last compliment
you gave someone?

_____

_____

_____

_____

_____

_____

_____

_____

_____

_____

_____

_____

_____

_____

_____

_____

_____

_____

_____

_____

_____

_____

_____

_____

_____

_____

_____

_____

_____

_____

_____

_____

_____

_____

_____

JUNE 10

What compliment has someone
recently given to you?

_____

_____

_____

_____

_____

_____

_____

_____

_____

_____

_____

_____

_____

_____

_____

_____

_____

_____

JUNE 11

One self-care activity you
could do while waiting is . . .

JUNE 12

What step have you taken recently or plan to take to simplify your life?

_____

_____

_____

_____

_____

_____

_____

_____

_____

_____

_____

_____

_____

_____

_____

_____

_____

_____

_____

_____

_____

JUNE 13

What are two of your
go-to healthy snacks?

_____

_____

_____

_____

_____

_____

_____

_____

_____

_____

_____

_____

_____

_____

_____

_____

_____

_____

_____

_____

_____

_____

_____

_____

_____

_____

_____

_____

_____

_____

_____

_____

_____

_____

_____

_____

_____

_____

_____

JUNE 14

If you were given a magazine
and asked to cut out pictures
that represent the vision
you have for your life,
what pictures would you cut out?

_____

_____

_____

_____

_____

_____

_____

_____

_____

_____

_____

_____

_____

_____

JUNE 15

When you were young
you probably had a stuffed animal
or security blanket.
What item brings you comfort now?

JUNE 16

What's saving your life right now?

JUNE 17

What's something you are debating on whether or not to do?

_____

_____
_____
_____
_____
_____
_____
_____
_____
_____
_____
_____
_____
_____
_____
_____
_____
_____
_____

JUNE 18

If you could give your younger self a
piece of advice what would it be?

_____

_____

_____

_____

_____

_____

_____

_____

_____

_____

_____

_____

_____

_____

_____

_____

_____

_____

JUNE 19

Was there ever a time where
everything you hoped would happen
actually did?

JUNE 20

Name a person
that inspires you right now.

JUNE 21

What's something that you are shocked that you didn't see coming?

_____

_____

_____

_____

_____

_____

_____

_____

_____

_____

_____

_____

_____

_____

_____

_____

_____

_____

_____

_____

_____

_____

_____

_____

_____

_____

_____

_____

_____

_____

_____

_____

_____

_____

_____

_____

_____

_____

JUNE 22

What was the
biggest lesson
you learned this week?

JUNE 23

Where do you find
inspiration to be healthy?

JUNE 24

On a scale of 0-10
how happy are you right now
and why?

_____

_____

_____

_____

_____

_____

_____

_____

_____

_____

_____

_____

_____

_____

_____

_____

_____

_____

_____

JUNE 25

What's one habit you are trying to subtract from your life?

_____

_____

_____

_____

_____

_____

_____

_____

_____

_____

_____

_____

_____

_____

_____

_____

_____

_____

_____

_____

_____

_____

_____

_____

_____

_____

_____

_____

_____

_____

_____

_____

_____

_____

_____

JUNE 26

What's one habit
you are trying to
add to your life?

_____

_____

_____

_____

_____

_____

_____

_____

_____

_____

_____

_____

_____

_____

_____

_____

_____

_____

_____

JUNE 27

Today you are grateful for . . .

JUNE 28

What do you crave in your life that doesn't exist today?

_____

_____

_____

_____

_____

_____

_____

_____

_____

_____

_____

_____

_____

_____

_____

_____

_____

_____

_____

_____

JUNE 29

How could you rearrange your day to
prioritize your health & happiness?

JUNE 30

What keeps you from asking
for help with some of
your tasks & responsibilities?

JULY 1

What things or people
give you strength?

_____

_____

_____

_____

_____

_____

_____

_____

_____

_____

_____

_____

_____

_____

_____

_____

_____

_____

_____

_____

JULY 2

What something healthy you enjoy that also feels like a treat?

_____

_____

_____

_____

_____

_____

_____

_____

_____

_____

_____

_____

_____

_____

_____

_____

JULY 3

What's your favorite thing about
summer?

JULY 4

The best advice you ever
received was . . .

JULY 5

Name one place you've always
wanted to visit.

_____

_____

_____

_____

_____

_____

_____

_____

_____

_____

_____

_____

_____

_____

_____

_____

_____

JULY 6

How could you strengthen
your support system?

_____

_____

_____

_____

_____

_____

_____

_____

_____

_____

_____

_____

_____

_____

_____

_____

JULY 7

How do you cope with a difficult day?

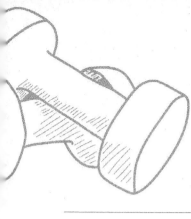

JULY 8

What's one thing you did today to prioritize your own health and wellness?

_____

_____

_____

_____

_____

_____

_____

_____

_____

_____

_____

_____

_____

_____

_____

_____

_____

_____

JULY 9

Share something that is keeping you up at night (and then cross it out!).

_____
_____
_____
_____
_____
_____
_____
_____
_____
_____
_____
_____
_____
_____
_____
_____
_____
_____
_____
_____

JULY 10

Share about a time or place
when you felt
completely at peace.

_____

_____

_____

_____

_____

_____

_____

_____

_____

_____

_____

_____

_____

_____

JULY 11

Where would you like to visit in your
dream tonight?

JULY 12

If your best friend asked you
what to do to relieve stress,
you would tell them to . . .

JULY 13

Which emojis would you pick to describe your day?

_____
_____
_____
_____
_____
_____
_____
_____
_____
_____
_____
_____
_____
_____
_____
_____
_____
_____
_____
_____
_____
_____

JULY 14

Describe the ingredients
in your favorite salad.

_____

_____

_____

_____

_____

_____

_____

_____

_____

_____

_____

_____

_____

_____

_____

JULY 15

What are you looking forward
to doing this week?

JULY 16

What self care wisdom
would you share with a friend
who is on the road to burnout?

_____

_____

_____

_____

_____

_____

_____

_____

_____

_____

_____

_____

_____

_____

_____

_____

_____

_____

JULY 17

What is the best thing that has happened to you this week?

hello

_____

_____

_____

_____

_____

_____

_____

_____

_____

_____

_____

_____

_____

_____

_____

_____

_____

_____

_____

_____

_____

_____

_____

_____

_____

_____

_____

_____

_____

_____

_____

_____

_____

_____

_____

JULY 18

What activity
do you find
to be therapeutic?

_____

_____

_____

_____

_____

_____

_____

_____

_____

_____

_____

_____

_____

_____

JULY 19

Share a boundary that you set
(or need to set)
to create more
me time for yourself?

JULY 20

In what ways could your family members help take something off your plate?

_____

_____

_____

_____

_____

_____

_____

_____

_____

_____

_____

_____

_____

_____

_____

_____

_____

_____

_____

_____

_____

JULY 21

Designate a date next week
for family night.

What activity will you enjoy
doing together?

_____

_____

_____

_____

_____

_____

_____

_____

_____

_____

_____

_____

_____

_____

_____

_____

_____

_____

_____

_____

_____

_____

_____

_____

_____

_____

_____

_____

_____

_____

_____

_____

_____

_____

_____

_____

JULY 22

Name one creative way
you could
squeeze a few minutes
of physical activity into your day.

JULY 23

Who could you ask for help
that you haven't reached out to yet?

In what specific way
could they assist you?

JULY 24

Do you feel like you are 'enough'?

Why or why not?

_____

_____

_____

_____

_____

_____

_____

_____

_____

_____

_____

_____

_____

_____

_____

_____

_____

_____

_____

_____

_____

JULY 25

Currently your life feels
balanced/unbalanced
because . . .

_____

_____

_____

_____

_____

_____

_____

_____

_____

_____

_____

_____

_____

_____

_____

_____

_____

_____

_____

_____

_____

_____

_____

_____

_____

_____

_____

_____

_____

_____

_____

_____

_____

_____

_____

_____

_____

_____

_____

JULY 26

What's something
you are really good at?

_____

_____

_____

_____

_____

_____

_____

_____

_____

_____

_____

_____

_____

_____

_____

_____

_____

JULY 27

What's your latest
go-to quick
and healthy meal?

JULY 28

Share a goal you are currently working on and why it's important to you.

JULY 29

Who are the 5 people
you spend the most time with?

Do they lift you up or tear you down?

_____

_____

_____

_____

_____

_____

_____

_____

_____

_____

_____

_____

_____

_____

_____

_____

_____

JULY 30

What courageous/difficult
conversation do you need
to have with someone?

JULY 31

What would need to be true
for you to share your story?

THINGS
to do

THINGS
to buy/have

THINGS
to be

PLACES
to go

AUGUST 1

If you could make a living doing
ANYTHING . . . what would you do?

_____

_____

_____

_____

_____

_____

_____

_____

_____

_____

_____

_____

_____

_____

_____

_____

_____

_____

_____

_____

AUGUST 2

Share about today
to capture
a single day in your life.

_____

_____

_____

_____

_____

_____

_____

_____

_____

_____

_____

_____

_____

_____

_____

AUGUST 3

Who has helped shape
the person you are today?

Have you told them what impact
they have had on your life?

AUGUST 4

What's something that you were afraid
to do and did it anyway?

AUGUST 5

In what way did a loss of something
or someone transform you?

_____

_____

_____

_____

_____

_____

_____

_____

_____

_____

_____

_____

_____

_____

_____

_____

_____

_____

_____

_____

_____

AUGUST 6

In general,
what's your self-care plan?

_____

_____

_____

_____

_____

_____

_____

_____

_____

_____

_____

_____

_____

_____

_____

_____

AUGUST 7

Where do you turn for support
in a difficult situation?

AUGUST 8

If someone told you self-care was
selfish, you would say . . .

_____

_____

_____

_____

_____

_____

_____

_____

_____

_____

_____

_____

_____

_____

_____

_____

_____

_____

_____

AUGUST 9

What kind of mental activities do you enjoy that keep your mind sharp?

_____

_____

_____

_____

_____

_____

_____

_____

_____

_____

_____

_____

_____

_____

_____

_____

_____

_____

_____

_____

_____

_____

_____

_____

_____

_____

_____

_____

_____

_____

_____

_____

_____

_____

_____

_____

_____

_____

AUGUST 10

In what ways do you
deepen and nurture
your spiritual
connection?

_____

_____

_____

_____

_____

_____

_____

_____

_____

_____

_____

_____

_____

_____

_____

_____

_____

AUGUST 11

Why is it worth taking the time to
make your self-care a priority?

AUGUST 12

How would taking better care
of yourself have a positive impact
on your life and those around you?

_____

_____

_____

_____

_____

_____

_____

_____

_____

_____

_____

_____

_____

_____

_____

_____

_____

_____

_____

AUGUST 13

What makes you feel nurtured,
pampered or just plain good?

_____

_____

_____

_____

_____

_____

_____

_____

_____

_____

_____

_____

_____

_____

_____

_____

_____

_____

_____

_____

AUGUST 14

What everyday activity
do you find to be
therapeutic?

ZZZ

_____

_____

_____

_____

_____

_____

_____

_____

_____

_____

_____

_____

_____

_____

_____

_____

_____

_____

_____

_____

_____

AUGUST 15

What do you value
most in this world?

Are you spending your time
on the things you value?

AUGUST 16

What obstacles are getting in the way
of your health and happiness?

What could you do to eliminate some
of these obstacles?

AUGUST 17

What positive expectation do you
have for tomorrow?

_____

_____

_____

_____

_____

_____

_____

_____

_____

_____

_____

_____

_____

_____

_____

_____

_____

_____

_____

_____

_____

_____

_____

_____

_____

_____

_____

_____

_____

_____

_____

_____

_____

_____

_____

_____

AUGUST 18

What was the best thing
that happened to you today?

_____
_____
_____
_____
_____
_____
_____
_____
_____
_____
_____
_____
_____
_____

AUGUST 19

What kind of liquids do you
put in your body?

What systems could you put in place
to drink more water?

AUGUST 20

What types of silence inducing
activities may help reduce the noise
in your life (e.g. meditation, prayer,
gratification)?

AUGUST 21

Close your eyes and picture
something good
happening in your life.

What did you visualize?

_____

_____

_____

_____

_____

_____

_____

_____

_____

_____

_____

_____

_____

_____

_____

_____

_____

_____

_____

_____

_____

_____

_____

_____

_____

_____

_____

_____

_____

_____

_____

_____

_____

_____

_____

AUGUST 22

What's something
most people
don't know about you?

_____

_____

_____

_____

_____

_____

_____

_____

_____

_____

_____

_____

_____

_____

_____

_____

_____

_____

AUGUST 23

What is something you do
that makes you feel
confident or invincible?

AUGUST 24

You spend most of your time
thinking about . . .

_____
_____
_____
_____
_____
_____
_____
_____
_____
_____
_____
_____
_____
_____
_____
_____
_____
_____
_____
_____

AUGUST 25

What activity were you last doing where you lost track of time because you were in the zone?

_____

_____

_____

_____

_____

_____

_____

_____

_____

_____

_____

_____

_____

_____

_____

_____

_____

_____

_____

_____

_____

_____

_____

_____

_____

_____

_____

_____

_____

_____

_____

_____

_____

_____

_____

_____

_____

_____

_____

_____

AUGUST 26

You won the lottery!

What changes would you
first make to your life and
how you spend your time?

AUGUST 27

What would you do
or try if you knew
you could not fail?

AUGUST 28

When was the last time you couldn't sleep because you were so excited about something?

_____
_____
_____
_____
_____
_____
_____
_____
_____
_____
_____
_____
_____
_____
_____
_____
_____
_____
_____
_____
_____

AUGUST 29

What positive habit could you
incorporate when you
stop at a red light
or when a TV commercial comes on?

_____
_____
_____
_____
_____
_____
_____
_____
_____
_____
_____
_____
_____
_____
_____
_____
_____

_____

_____

_____

_____

_____

_____

_____

_____

_____

_____

_____

_____

_____

_____

_____

_____

AUGUST 30

What was the last success
you had?

How did you celebrate
and reward yourself?

_____

_____

_____

_____

_____

_____

_____

_____

_____

_____

_____

_____

_____

_____

_____

_____

AUGUST 31

Are you up to date on all
your personal wellness visits?

If not, which appointments
do you need to make?

_____'s

Self Care Plan

SPIRIT	**HEART**
BODY	**MIND**

MY TRIBE OF HELPERS

SEPTEMBER 1

What natural gifts and talents do you appreciate about yourself?

_____

_____

_____

_____

_____

_____

_____

_____

_____

_____

_____

_____

_____

_____

_____

_____

_____

_____

SEPTEMBER 2

What is something you recently
realized you had no control over
and eventually let go of?

SEPTEMBER 3

Do you enjoy and believe
in the work you are doing?

SEPTEMBER 4

In what setting do you tend to feel more relaxed?

SEPTEMBER 5

You couldn't imagine
a world without . . .

SEPTEMBER 6

What's something you could
do today that your future self
would thank you for?

_____

_____

_____

_____

_____

_____

_____

_____

_____

_____

_____

_____

_____

_____

_____

SEPTEMBER 7

List a few date night activities that
would be fun to do with your partner?

SEPTEMBER 8

What's an excuse that you are hanging on to that is holding you back?

Write it down and then cross it out!

_____

_____

_____

_____

_____

_____

_____

_____

_____

_____

_____

_____

_____

_____

_____

_____

_____

_____

_____

_____

SEPTEMBER 9

In what ways do you combat loneliness or isolation?

_____

_____

_____

_____

_____

_____

_____

_____

_____

_____

_____

_____

_____

_____

_____

_____

_____

_____

_____

_____

_____

_____

_____

_____

_____

_____

_____

_____

_____

_____

_____

_____

_____

_____

_____

_____

SEPTEMBER 10

What are some ideas
you have to slow down
and enjoy life more?

_____

_____

_____

_____

_____

_____

_____

_____

_____

_____

_____

_____

_____

_____

_____

_____

SEPTEMBER 11

How do you incorporate technology
into your healthy habits?

SEPTEMBER 12

What do others need to know about
your end of life preferences?

SEPTEMBER 13

What is something for you that you are currently praying for?

_____

_____

_____

_____

_____

_____

_____

_____

_____

_____

_____

_____

_____

_____

_____

_____

_____

_____

_____

SEPTEMBER 14

You deserve happiness
because . . .

SEPTEMBER 15

What smells energize you?

SEPTEMBER 16

Share a recent experience where you felt drained or depleted.

Is there anything you could have done differently to prevent these feelings?

_____

_____

_____

_____

_____

_____

_____

_____

_____

_____

_____

_____

_____

_____

_____

_____

_____

_____

SEPTEMBER 17

What experiences from your past are potentially weighing you down?

_____

_____

_____

_____

_____

_____

_____

_____

_____

_____

_____

_____

_____

_____

_____

_____

_____

SEPTEMBER 18

What's one small thing
you could change
that would result
in a positive ripple effect
in your life?

_____

_____

_____

_____

_____

_____

_____

_____

_____

_____

_____

_____

_____

_____

_____

_____

SEPTEMBER 19

What tiny moments
in your day
are having a big impact
on your life?

SEPTEMBER 20

What new skills
would you like to develop?

SEPTEMBER 21

Count your blessings.

List out a few of the blessings in your life.

_____

_____

_____

_____

_____

_____

_____

_____

_____

_____

_____

_____

_____

_____

_____

_____

_____

_____

_____

_____

_____

_____

_____

_____

_____

_____

_____

_____

_____

_____

_____

_____

_____

_____

_____

_____

SEPTEMBER 22

In what ways could you be more
intentional with your health and
happiness desires?

_____

_____

_____

_____

_____

_____

_____

_____

_____

_____

_____

_____

_____

_____

_____

SEPTEMBER 23

What space in your home
feels like (or could feel like)
a little oasis?

SEPTEMBER 24

What hurdle have you recently overcame?

_____
_____
_____
_____
_____
_____
_____
_____
_____
_____
_____
_____
_____
_____
_____
_____
_____
_____
_____
_____
_____

SEPTEMBER 25

What are some sounds that you enjoy?

_____

_____

_____

_____

_____

_____

_____

_____

_____

_____

_____

_____

_____

_____

_____

_____

_____

SEPTEMBER 26

What is something you are
procrastinating
that would bring you
more health and happiness?

_____

_____

_____

_____

_____

_____

_____

_____

_____

_____

_____

_____

_____

_____

_____

_____

_____

_____

SEPTEMBER 27

Define what
being strong
looks and feels like.

SEPTEMBER 28

What foods do you consume that
make you feel energized?

_____

_____

_____

_____

_____

_____

_____

_____

_____

_____

_____

_____

_____

_____

_____

_____

_____

_____

_____

_____

SEPTEMBER 29

What are some of your
favorite power words?

Tip: Use these as some of your
online passwords!

SEPTEMBER 30

What's one thing
you say to yourself
that you wouldn't say
to your best friend?

OCTOBER 1

Describe what a happier and healthier version of you would look like.

_____

_____

_____

_____

_____

_____

_____

_____

_____

_____

_____

_____

_____

_____

_____

_____

_____

_____

_____

_____

_____

_____

_____

_____

_____

_____

_____

_____

_____

_____

_____

_____

_____

_____

_____

_____

_____

OCTOBER 2

You feel happiest
when you are . . .

OCTOBER 3

What's a life lesson that you believe
needs to be taught in school?

OCTOBER 4

What do you believe
you deserve in your life?

_____

_____

_____

_____

_____

_____

_____

_____

_____

_____

_____

_____

_____

_____

_____

_____

_____

OCTOBER 5

What does love mean to you?

How do you show these emotions and actions to yourself?

_____

_____

_____

_____

_____

_____

_____

_____

_____

_____

_____

_____

_____

_____

_____

_____

_____

_____

_____

_____

_____

OCTOBER 6

You forgive yourself for . . .

_____

_____

_____

_____

_____

_____

_____

_____

_____

_____

_____

_____

_____

_____

_____

_____

_____

OCTOBER 7

Describe what you want to be true
in your life at this time next year.

OCTOBER 8

What's your favorite thing about fall?

_____

_____

_____

_____

_____

_____

_____

_____

_____

_____

_____

_____

_____

_____

_____

_____

_____

_____

_____

OCTOBER 9

What's currently keeping
you awake at night?

_____
_____
_____
_____
_____
_____
_____
_____
_____
_____
_____
_____
_____
_____
_____
_____
_____
_____
_____
_____

_____

_____

_____

_____

_____

_____

_____

_____

_____

_____

_____

_____

_____

_____

_____

_____

_____

_____

_____

_____

OCTOBER 10

Share something
that is holding you back
from being more authentic.

_____

_____

_____

_____

_____

_____

_____

_____

_____

_____

_____

_____

_____

_____

_____

_____

OCTOBER 11

How many hours of solitude
do you need to optimally function
and feel happy?

OCTOBER 12

In what ways may you be currently sabotaging your own health and happiness?

_____

_____

_____

_____

_____

_____

_____

_____

_____

_____

_____

_____

_____

_____

_____

_____

_____

_____

_____

_____

OCTOBER 13

Do you currently feel supported by your family and friends?

Why? Or why not?

_____
_____
_____
_____
_____
_____
_____
_____
_____
_____
_____
_____
_____
_____
_____
_____
_____
_____

_____

_____

_____

_____

_____

_____

_____

_____

_____

_____

_____

_____

_____

_____

_____

_____

_____

_____

_____

OCTOBER 14

Do you have any regrets
about your life so far?

If so, what changes could you make
so you live a life without regret?

_____

_____

_____

_____

_____

_____

_____

_____

_____

_____

_____

_____

_____

_____

_____

_____

_____

OCTOBER 15

What important need do you have
right now that isn't being met?

OCTOBER 16

How could you prevent from being caught up in other people's problems?

_____

_____

_____

_____

_____

_____

_____

_____

_____

_____

_____

_____

_____

_____

_____

_____

_____

_____

_____

_____

_____

OCTOBER 17

How is your inner critic potentially
stopping you from moving forward?

_____

_____

_____

_____

_____

_____

_____

_____

_____

_____

_____

_____

_____

_____

_____

_____

_____

_____

_____

_____

_____

_____

_____

_____

_____

_____

_____

_____

_____

_____

_____

_____

_____

_____

_____

_____

_____

OCTOBER 18

What did your teenage self
imagine you'd be doing right now?

_____
_____
_____
_____
_____
_____
_____
_____
_____
_____
_____
_____
_____
_____
_____
_____

OCTOBER 19

What do other people
always thank you for?

OCTOBER 20

If you had to leave your house all day,
every day, where would you go and
what would you do?

_____

_____

_____

_____

_____

_____

_____

_____

_____

_____

_____

_____

_____

_____

_____

_____

_____

_____

_____

_____

OCTOBER 21

Your favorite daily ritual is . . .

_____

_____

_____

_____

_____

_____

_____

_____

_____

_____

_____

_____

_____

_____

_____

_____

_____

_____

_____

OCTOBER 22

How would you
spend your time
if you didn't care
what others thought?

OCTOBER 23

What sparks your creative side?

OCTOBER 24

What's a quote, saying,
or verse that inspires you?

OCTOBER 25

What do you want more of in your life?

hello

_____

_____

_____

_____

_____

_____

_____

_____

_____

_____

_____

_____

_____

_____

_____

_____

_____

_____

OCTOBER 26

How would you
describe a successful life?

_____

_____

_____

_____

_____

_____

_____

_____

_____

_____

_____

_____

_____

_____

_____

_____

_____

_____

OCTOBER 27

What do you
geek out about?

OCTOBER 28

Reflect on a time you felt transformed.
How did you change and why?

OCTOBER 29

If you could time travel
back to another time,
where would you go?

OCTOBER 30

You can choose one superpower.

What would it be?

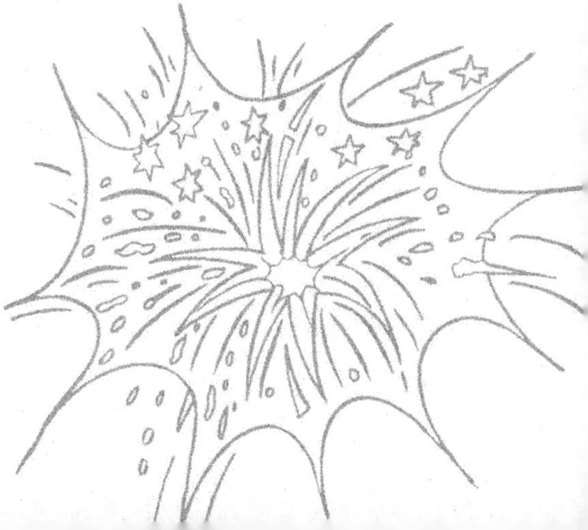

OCTOBER 31

List three things
that you have feared
and three things
that have comforted you.

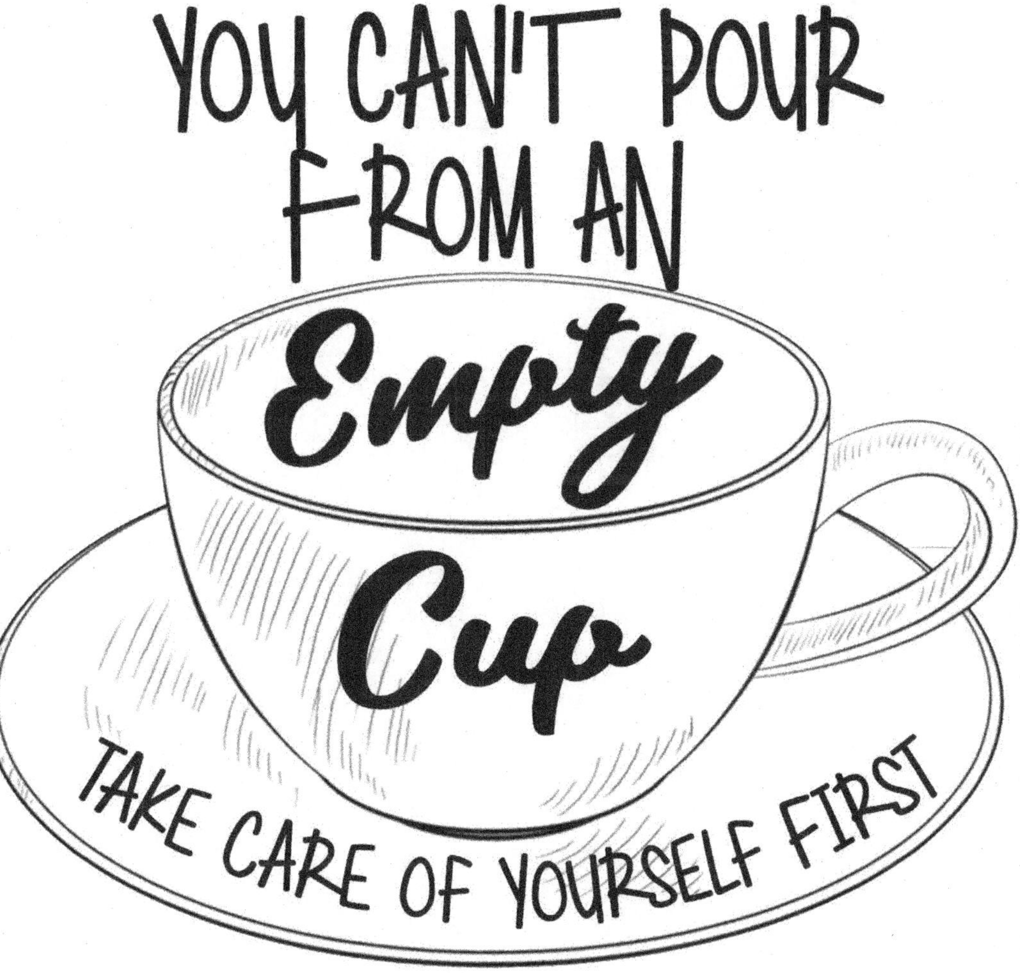
YOU CAN'T POUR
FROM AN
Empty
Cup
TAKE CARE OF YOURSELF FIRST

NOVEMBER 1

What's one thing
you keep telling yourself
you'll do when you have
more time or retire?

_____

_____

_____

_____

_____

_____

_____

_____

_____

_____

_____

_____

_____

_____

_____

_____

_____

_____

_____

_____

NOVEMBER 2

What's a charity that is important to you and why?

NOVEMBER 3

What's a secret passion you have
that you haven't shared with anyone?

NOVEMBER 4

Your signature color or a color
that makes you happy is . . .

_____

_____

_____

_____

_____

_____

_____

_____

_____

_____

_____

_____

_____

_____

_____

_____

_____

_____

_____

_____

NOVEMBER 5

List out the things you are
ridiculously good at.

NOVEMBER 6

What do you order
at your local coffee shop?

_____

_____

_____

_____

_____

_____

_____

_____

_____

_____

_____

_____

_____

_____

_____

_____

_____

_____

NOVEMBER 7

Who is one person you could thank for
being there when you needed it most?

NOVEMBER 8

What is your most treasured
possession and why?

_____

_____

_____

_____

_____

_____

_____

_____

_____

_____

_____

_____

_____

_____

_____

_____

_____

_____

_____

_____

NOVEMBER 9

What great things in the future
are you anticipating?

NOVEMBER 10

What change could you make
to your physical desk space
that would make it more inviting?

_____

_____

_____

_____

_____

_____

_____

_____

_____

_____

_____

_____

_____

_____

_____

_____

_____

NOVEMBER 11

What has surprised you
about your life so far?

NOVEMBER 12

What are you looking forward
to doing this week?

_____

_____

_____

_____

_____

_____

_____

_____

_____

_____

_____

_____

_____

_____

_____

_____

_____

_____

_____

_____

_____

_____

NOVEMBER 13

What's one thing you
accomplished today?

_____

_____

_____

_____

_____

_____

_____

_____

_____

_____

_____

_____

_____

_____

_____

_____

_____

_____

NOVEMBER 14

What's one of your
favorite indulgences?

_____

_____

_____

_____

_____

_____

_____

_____

_____

_____

_____

_____

_____

_____

_____

_____

_____

_____

NOVEMBER 15

When was the last time
you stepped out of
your comfort zone?

NOVEMBER 16

What is important to you
ethically or morally?

_____

_____

_____

_____

_____

_____

_____

_____

_____

_____

_____

_____

_____

_____

_____

_____

_____

_____

_____

_____

_____

_____

NOVEMBER 17

What's a limiting belief you have about yourself or your abilities?

NOVEMBER 18

What good habit
do you want to
begin this month?

NOVEMBER 19

Your evenings would be
more restful if . . .

NOVEMBER 20

How could you set
better boundaries in your life?

_____

_____

_____

_____

_____

_____

_____

_____

_____

_____

_____

_____

_____

_____

_____

_____

_____

_____

_____

_____

NOVEMBER 21

What is something you need to speak up about or ask for?

_____

NOVEMBER 22

How could you
give yourself a break today?

NOVEMBER 23

What blessing
surfaced during a difficult time?

NOVEMBER 24

How could you simplify your holiday season to allow you to be more present in the festivities?

_____

_____

_____

_____

_____

_____

_____

_____

_____

_____

_____

_____

_____

_____

_____

_____

_____

_____

_____

_____

NOVEMBER 25

What's a song that you can't help but get up and dance to?

_____

_____

_____

_____

_____

_____

_____

_____

_____

_____

_____

_____

_____

_____

_____

_____

_____

_____

NOVEMBER 26

What's the last book
you read that you
would recommend?

NOVEMBER 27

What do you love
about your personality?

NOVEMBER 28

What is your favorite holiday tradition you do with your family?

_____

_____

_____

_____

_____

_____

_____

_____

_____

_____

_____

_____

_____

_____

_____

_____

_____

_____

_____

_____

NOVEMBER 29

Are the social accounts you follow lifting you up or tearing you down?

NOVEMBER 30

Describe what a happy
and healthy person looks like.

DECEMBER 1

What was the last thing
you said 'no' or 'not now' to?

DECEMBER 2

Describe your favorite outdoor spot.

DECEMBER 3

Something people say which helps them be happier or healthier that you've never tried is . . .

DECEMBER 4

What characteristics
do you admire in a close friend?

Do you have these characteristics?

DECEMBER 5

How would you spend a day
you had all to yourself?

_____

DECEMBER 6

Looking ahead, your to-do list
this week may be overwhelming.

How do you make it more
manageable?

_____

_____

_____

_____

_____

_____

_____

_____

_____

_____

_____

_____

_____

_____

_____

_____

DECEMBER 7

What's one thing
you could do daily
to stop and give yourself a break?

DECEMBER 8

What are the moments that really
matter in your life right now?

DECEMBER 9

What is one thing you look
forward to every day?

_____

_____

_____

_____

_____

_____

_____

_____

_____

_____

_____

_____

_____

_____

_____

_____

_____

_____

DECEMBER 10

Write a few fun individual words
that when you hear them,
bring a smile to your face.

hello

_____

_____

_____

_____

_____

_____

_____

_____

_____

_____

_____

_____

_____

_____

_____

_____

_____

_____

DECEMBER 11

What plan could you put in place
to recharge when your energy is
depleted?

DECEMBER 12

Describe something
that you would invent.

DECEMBER 13

What's the most outrageous thing you have ever done?

DECEMBER 14

How do you
deal with anger?

DECEMBER 15

What is the dominant
emotion in your life right now?

DECEMBER 16

What was the last great idea
you had in the shower
or on a solo car ride?

_____

_____

_____

_____

_____

_____

_____

_____

_____

_____

_____

_____

_____

_____

_____

_____

_____

DECEMBER 17

The holiday tradition
you look forward to is . . .

DECEMBER 18

If you could be famous
for something
what would you want
to be famous for?

_____

_____

_____

_____

_____

_____

_____

_____

_____

_____

_____

_____

_____

_____

DECEMBER 19

What is the last
new thing you tried?

DECEMBER 20

What's one thing you did just for
yourself today?

DECEMBER 21

What would you ask for if a genie granted you three wishes?

_____

_____

_____

_____

_____

_____

_____

_____

_____

_____

_____

_____

_____

_____

_____

_____

_____

_____

_____

_____

_____

_____

_____

_____

_____

_____

_____

_____

_____

_____

_____

_____

_____

_____

_____

_____

_____

DECEMBER 22

What are some of the
quirky things about you
that make you endearing?

DECEMBER 23

What would make you
feel spiritually fulfilled?

DECEMBER 24

What's something good you have
inherited from your mom or dad?

_____

_____

_____

_____

_____

_____

_____

_____

_____

_____

_____

_____

_____

_____

_____

_____

DECEMBER 25

Something you enjoyed
doing with your parents
when you were little was . . .

_____

_____

_____

_____

_____

_____

_____

_____

_____

_____

_____

_____

_____

_____

_____

_____

_____

_____

_____

_____

_____

DECEMBER 26

What did you eat today?

DECEMBER 27

How do you get the
intellectual stimulation
you need?

DECEMBER 28

Write your self a little love note.

DECEMBER 29

What are you currently searching for?

DECEMBER 30

Doodle something
in the space above . . .
maybe a doodle
you did as a kid.

_____

_____

_____

_____

_____

_____

_____

_____

_____

_____

_____

_____

_____

_____

_____

_____

_____

_____

DECEMBER 31

What positive changes
have happened to you
in the last year?

Winter WORKOUT

1 minute plank

2 burpees

3 leg lifts

4 backward lunges

5 push-ups

6 forward lunges

7 tricep dips

8 squats

9 sit-ups

10 mountain climbers

11 air bicycles

12 jumping jacks

MEMORIES

JANUARY	FEBRUARY	MARCH
APRIL	MAY	JUNE
JULY	AUGUST	SEPTEMBER
OCTOBER	NOVEMBER	DECEMBER

"Good times come and go, but the memories last forever..."

Self-Care WORD SEARCH

```
G Q I L Y C C I F R J O C U P N X G H D S I W U Y
Z M U S I C D N C L J U M R Z L B N J O Z R V G Q
S O Z F S L C Y N B V W M I N D F U L N E S S R Z
H E A L T H Y Z R S W E E I D N I L B Y U J Z S A
O G Q Q T G O P K G V U L P R L N U T R I T I O N
N S V L G A D F C G W Y Z R T O I N Q V U J T B O
N E E X Z Y V F C E K V H S H I O V D T J H H V E
X L B P G I Q I C P C O M P A S S I O N W Z Z Q Y
Q F S L Z R G U G H V F P D O Z L Q U V S B G D V
N C H H G Y A I Y U O T R L A U G H T E R M A R Y
T A O Q X W F T N K I B S I S L D N M K G L S E N
P R U Y M P X Z I T C E B Q E Y D Z X O X L K A A
U E K Y O F H U Z T E P F I R N T C G T U B F M K
O K T D V J T S B L U N Q I E P D O N J G O O S P
B P P F E F D S C H Y D T R B S O S K N Y D R O S
V Z P T M O I K S U A X E I I H T F E C P Y H R K
E M T U E K C Q L W M P V Y O S W N N W N I E S J
Y S X U N T A S E T V I P B X N Y I A H I M L A K
U U V R T J L G E M A B C I W J A M B A M A P S Q
A P J R D I M G P O O S B Y N O B L O A U G B B V
Y P H I B U A C O Y U J R S A E B O V L Z E E Z I
M O O C S B S D S M Z T Q K K Z S D D V Z L Q O H
G R W B M R Q E D P R S D N D N R S M J R U U G M
W T M J O I Q P K O B W Y X U C Q X P L A M Y E P
R A M J I L C F Q H M D X D K E R U N P L U G Z R
```

intentional	mindfulness	ask for help	compassion
body-image	nutrition	gratitude	happiness
self-care	movement	hobbies	laughter
healthy	friends	support	unplug
sleep	music	dreams	calm

ABOUT THE AUTHOR

Elizabeth Miller is a wife, mother, full-time employee, family caregiver and Certified Caregiving Consultant. She obtained a B.A. in Journalism from Penn State University and has worked in software development and strategy for almost 20 years. Elizabeth's personal experiences caring for aging parents with chronic and terminal illnesses as well as caring for a sibling with developmental disabilities inspired her to create Happy Healthy Caregiver in 2015. Through her consulting services, resources, and online community, Elizabeth helps family caregivers integrate caregiving with their busy lives.

Elizabeth has been a presenter at the annual National Caregiving Conferences. Her story has been featured in Woman's Day and the Marietta Daily Journal. She is also the host of the Happy Healthy Caregiver podcast on the Whole Care Network, a freelance writer, and facilitates an Atlanta support group for family caregivers called the Atlanta Daughterhood Circle.

✉ elizabeth@happyhealthycaregiver.com

🌐 happyhealthycaregiver.com

📷 happyhealthycaregiver

f happyhealthycaregiver

🐦 HHCaregiver

in elizabethbmiller

ABOUT HAPPY HEALTHY CAREGIVER

Happy Healthy Caregiver is a lifestyle website and podcast helping family caregivers create time for what they love and be intentional with self-care while juggling the responsibilities of caregiving.

All of the resources available through Happy Healthy Caregiver teach and encourage self-care for the caregiver. Posts, podcast episodes, and instructional training materials help family caregivers make small healthy changes, reclaim their time, ask others for help, express their emotions and needs, revitalize self-interests, and better understand care resources and options.

Our mission is to help caregivers all over the world become happier and healthier while caring for others. We can do hard things but we don't need to do them alone.